Special Woman

Debbie Gumede

Special Woman

ISBN: 978-0-620-66246-8

CONTENTS

FOREWORD

"Special woman,   there is a value God has placed upon you as an individual
Think and talk as someone special . Walk and live as someone special
Because you are special"

"Your life is God's gift to you; Enjoy every moment of your life;
Challenge yourself to live your best life now, conscious that you are special, unique and truly loved by God"

You are God's best and God thinks so highly of you.
I pray that you will let this truth sink so deep in your spirit and soul and allow it to influence the decisions you make in life.

I pray that you will realize that you are a treasure so precious to God today and always. You deserve the best in every area of your life and that is why God made provisions for you for such a life in and through the Lord Jesus Christ. Jesus loves you!

DEDICATION

As a woman I have been blessed to have special women in my life, women who have been there for me through the different seasons of my life.

The following women stand out and I truly pray that their love for me will be greatly rewarded by the Lord Almighty.

Felistas Gano, my mum, was an amazing woman whose inner strength was incredible. She was delicate like any woman but who said being feminine is equivalent to weakness? It's only when I became a woman that I realized that my mum was a real blessing and a woman of inner strength and beauty. I honour and celebrate her life through this book and the following women because of who they are, but more so, because of their devotion to God:

Sylvia Msimanga, Elizabeth Gumede, Bongi Baker, Boni Chinhara, Mabel Marisa, Maureen Mnkandla, Petunia Chiriseri, Cynthia Kuppusami, Cynthia Sande, Paidamoyo Matongoti, Felicity Karekwaivanani, Deborah Gano, Eppy Gano and Celia Svosve.

As a woman you need to know the treasure that you carry inside you and allow the God who put it inside you to use it to enrich your world. You are no ordinary woman and I pray that as you read these few pages, you will be blessed and allow the blessing of God to flow out of you to the other women around you.

You are a special woman.

Psalm 139[14] I will praise you (Lord), for I am fearfully and wonderfully made; marvelous are your works, and that my soul knows very well!

ACKNOWLEDGMENTS

Special acknowledgement goes to my best-friend who has become a sister to me over the years, Paidamoyo Matongoti. She has shared with me her life and has shared in all my joys, battles and tears and remained true. I love her dearly and will always cherish my relationship with her.

I also want to acknowledge my editor, Epiphania Gano. I treasure her input and encouragement and the time she invested in making this book possible.

My husband Thobile has always wanted to see all of my dreams come true. He once asked me, 'what stops you from writing?' and I replied, 'a dreary environment', to which he replied, 'then create the environment that inspires you'. I did just that and was able to write this book and I enjoyed every moment of it

Prayer of Salvation

John 3: 16
For God so loved the world that He gave his only Son that whoever
believes in him should not perish but have eternal life.

The invitation to have a genuine relationship with the Lord Jesus Christ is
for whoever. If you have not yet made that decision to have a personal
relationship with Jesus, you have an opportunity to do so.

Jesus loves you and He loves you very much.
Jesus is the answer to all human problems and it's only when you have
this relationship with Jesus Christ that you live life as God always planned
it for you.

If you do not yet have a personal relationship with Jesus Christ and you
want to have one with him, say this prayer with me:

O LORD God, I believe with all my heart that Jesus Christ is the Son of
God.
I believe he died for me and God raised him from the dead. I believe He is
alive today.
I confess with my mouth that Jesus Christ is the Lord of my life from
today.
Through him and in his name I have eternal life. I am born again.
Thank you Lord, for saving me
I am now a child of God. Hallelujah

Congratulations

Now that you are born again:

i. Realize you are now a new creature (literally) with no past - all things have become new 2 Corinthians 5:17
ii. Start feeding your spirit daily with the Word of God - Joshua 1:8
iii. Find a good bible-based church ad fellowship with the family of God. You are now a member of His body - the church
iv. Share the good news of your salvation with others in your world and finally
v. Live your life to the full- it is for this that Jesus came - so that you may have life and have it to the full John 10:10

God bless you

Special Woman

Special Woman

Special Woman

Special Woman

CHAPTER 1

"It's just the beginning"

Just because things didn't go the way you had planned, doesn't mean you must be discouraged and distraught about life.

God allows certain doors to close for a purpose.

At times we are quick to complain because we do not see the bigger picture but before we complain and lose hope let's turn to God.

Take the time to reflect on where you have been, how far you have come and all the goodness that surrounds you. There are some doors, should they remain open, you will never reach your full potential in life.

There are some doors that we keep open because they offer us a sense of security but not growth. They give us sustenance but not fulfillment.

When these doors close, it is opportunity to grow and venture into newness. It is opportunity for new beginnings that will usher you to become all that you were designed to become.

It's not time to look over your shoulder and cry over the doors you are leaving behind. It is time to celebrate new beginnings.

You don't need champagne to celebrate, simply start by putting a smile on your face and acknowledge the bright future that lies ahead.

Back up your confidence by calling your friend and telling them your destiny has just begun to unfold.

You don't need to have a detailed account on how your destiny is going to unfold. Believe it within you and be willing to take the first step, then destiny will show up and the world will see for itself that you are a woman with a purpose.

Your inner beauty will be revealed and usually that inner beauty will come with an inner strength that will radiate on the outside.

You are a carrier of greatness and God is waiting to unleash that greatness inside you. By nature you have the ability to conceive, to nurture and to give birth to greatness.

Rise up woman and walk into your destiny.

Jeremiah 29:11 "For I know the plans I have for you", declares the Lord, "plans to prosper you and not to harm you, plans to give you a hope and a future.

CHAPTER 2

"Hope in high heels"

Defeat usually dictates that you should remove your shoes and throw in the towel.

Success on the other hand doesn't give up easily.

When you have failed, it's not time to throw in the towel, but instead it's time to dress up for success. Put on your high heels and stand tall.

Rise above the present circumstance and tell yourself you are accepting nothing less but success. You can say this and say it with confidence because greater is He who is in you than he who is in the world. Yes, the Spirit of God in you cannot be defeated, so neither can you.

Consider how God came through for the Israelites – You are as precious to God as they were back then.

Confronted with the Red Sea before them and the Egyptian army in pursuit behind them, the Israelites could not cower and accept defeat. Some might have murmured because they did not know their God but Moses knew his God.

Defeat was not an option because defeat is also never your option as long as you are alive and have the life of God in you.

The very fact that you can breathe in the air, is enough evidence that you have what it takes to succeed in life. Only a dead woman has no hope. Moses had a rod in his hand

and that was all God needed and you have inside of you everything it takes to be a success.

Find a mirror and take a good look at the woman who looks back at you. Look her in the eyes and see the determination in those eyes. Look beyond the doubts and worries in the eyes and see the beauty housed by those eyes.

You cannot deny yourself the opportunity to manifest the greatness within you.

Because of hope – and a willingness to allow God to be God, for the Israelites, God paved the waters into dry land. If the Creator could do it for the Israelites then, know without a doubt, that He is able to do it for you because you are precious.

If He is the same God who declares that apart from Him there is no other God, then, there is nothing He cannot do with you and for you.

See the image of the woman in the mirror. She is a woman who was born for success, a woman who doesn't give up and that woman is you. Keep your heels on, for you are going places you never thought possible, until now.

Isaiah 43^3 -For I am the Lord your God, the Holy One of Israel, your Saviour; ^{4}Since you are precious in My sight, you are honoured and I have loved you"

Bible Reference:
1 John 4 verse 4, Exodus 14 verse 13 – 22, Isaiah 45 verse 5 -6, 2 Peter 1:3

CHAPTER 3

"Oops I broke my nail ..."

Is it not strange how we never see it coming.

None of us plans for disappointment or discouragement. We never plan to hear that hurtful word and when it comes, it gets to our heart and leaves us bruised inside.

Sometimes we take it very badly and it leaves tears streaming down our cheeks. At times we are brave on the outside and to avoid tarnishing our make-up, we hold back the tears but we feel the pain where it hurts the most – deep down in our soul.

Life's sad moments can destroy us, but they can only destroy us when we allow them to do so.

Just as we can easily say, "Oops I broke my nail – I need another manicure", we can say the same when disappointment comes.

Instead of pining in our misery, throwing ourselves a pity-party to which we usually invite, "Miss 'Why Me' and Madam 'I Wish'," we can choose to put things into perspective.

We may not be responsible for what happens to us but we are responsible for how we react when bad things happen to us.

Beautiful Ruth did not plan to be a widow in her prime years but it happened. Left childless with nothing in terms of wealth, Ruth received a raw deal in life, but she didn't look at it that way. She looked at her life and realized that it had given her a mother and a true friend in Naomi her mother-in-law. She valued the elderly woman so much that she vowed to follow her wherever she went. Ruth worked her way to royalty simply because a broken nail didn't stop her from gleaning through the field and opening her treasure casket.

Virtuous woman, decide how you will respond and your emotions will follow suit. Decide to be serene as you pass through life's tragedies. Decide to find strength in the face of adversity. Decide to let go of things that are beyond your control.

Every good well-thought-out decision has a tremendous effect on your overall appearance as a woman. Good decisions have a way of radiating your true beauty which others seldom see and wish to possess for themselves.

Psalm 23:^{6}-Surely goodness and mercy shall follow me all the days of my life and I shall dwell in the house of the Lord forever.

Bible Reference:

Ruth 1 verse 4 -5, 16 -17, 2 verse 2 -3

CHAPTER 4

"Keep those lips glossy"

There's a proverb that says that a word fitly spoken is like apples of gold in settings of silver.

Every woman appreciates beautiful things in life. We yearn for the luxurious ornaments of life. If we could have it our way, we would be surrounded with beauty and be all glamorous day in and day out.

The good news is that you can – it's just that many do not know how.

So a certain woman had been brought before Jesus by her accusers. They had caught her in the act of adultery and it was a situation she could not talk her way out of. Embarrassed and left with a tit bit of dignity, she came face to face with Jesus. Her accusers condemned her and were ready to stone her, but the one who could have condemned her forgave her. Jesus asked the woman if no one had condemned her and indeed no one had condemned her.

The woman now has to choose. Does she believe and receive her total vindication or does she continue to condemn herself?

She was told to go and sin no more.

You probably have blundered but who hasn't? The power of moving forward is in the words you speak about yourself. You speak more to yourself than to anyone and it is the content of your self-talk that propels you forward or takes you backwards.

The more negative words you speak about yourself to yourself, the more dry and cracked your lips become. You need some lip gloss of the life-giving word of God. When your lips are glossy with words of life, words of hope, words of strength, words of love, then you are more inclined to succeed in life and beautiful things do come your way. By the words of our mouth we attract the kind of life we want.

Words always precede manifestation.

We become what we speak.

Our words shape our world.

Keep your lips glossy, for while luxuries might seem like a fairy tale now – you may just be wowed one of these days, finding yourself surrounded with the beautiful things of life as a result of the words you have been speaking.

Proverbs 18:^{21} Death and life are in the power of the tongue, and those who love it will eat its fruit

Bible Reference:

Proverbs 25 verse 11
John 8 verse 2 - 12

CHAPTER 5

"When the make-up is off"

Who is the woman behind the make-up?

Sometimes many women find it difficult and painful to confront reality in the face. To be true to yourself demands that you address all unpleasant issues, issues which need to be dealt with, once and for all. Such issues must be dealt with in order for you to progress in life. One of the key issues which every woman must address is the issue of forgiveness.

Forgiveness is very therapeutic and refreshing and yet it is not the easiest of things to do. Who is it that wronged you and you are still hurting over it? Who is it that spoke an unkind word and you have been holding onto that word until now?

Unforgiveness is a deadly disease and it is very deceptive. Not only is it deadly in that it can bring physical sickness to your body but it also leaves you dejected and emotionally sick.

Even if you are the one who was wronged and you are the victim, you must still forgive.

Unfortunately many times the people who hurt us are able to move on with their lives while we sit and wallow in our misery – recounting everything they did or said to hurt us.

You need to realize that by not forgiving those who wrong you and hurt you, you are chaining yourself down. You are blocking your victory and your breakthrough. You can stifle your own growth simply by failing to forgive.

When you have been hurt it's not the time to put make-up and go on as if it is well with your soul. Beautiful princess, when you have been hurt, wash out all the make-up and face reality.

Forgive the person who hurt you.

Sometimes it's the tears of pain that will wash away that make-up. It's ok to cry it out, but when you are done, forgive.

Say it aloud – "Lord I forgive so and so". If possible – let the person know that you have forgiven them. You do not need to go into the details. Forgiving is for your own benefit. It releases you. It empowers you as an individual and diffuses the power of bitterness in your soul.

True natural beauty can only be seen when the make-up is off, sometimes we look much better without the layers of make-up.

Ephesians 4:^{32} -Be tenderhearted, forgiving one another, even as God in Christ forgave you

Bible Reference:

Matthew 6 verse 12 -14

CHAPTER 6

"The fragrance that lasts all day"

Every woman knows the power of a right fragrance for the occasion. An energizing fragrance can dramatically change a dreary mood into a robust mood. It can invigorate and revitalize you physically.

Attitude has the same effect on your environment and on you as a woman. A positive attitude works wonders and puts a bounce in your step.

Attitude is everything and you can have complete control over it. Before you react to anything there is actually room to decide how you will react. It can be a split second but it's there. The reason why it remains so small in proportion is because it is seldom exercised.

Instead of snarling when you drop something by mistake, laugh it off and give it an –oops! response. Instead of frowning and increasing the wrinkle lines on your brow, choose to smile and release some positive energy.

It sounds so trivial to think that such a small thing as attitude can make a difference but it does. With a positive attitude you are able to look at life from the perspective of a winner and not a loser. You are able to see yourself as a victor and not a victim. You are able to dance in the rain while another may be grumbling about a messed hair-do from the rain.

With the right attitude you can achieve more in your day and find more joy that every day becomes a day worth living.

There's nothing that brightens a woman's face like a beautiful smile and somehow a smile can put you in the right attitude. It's not the curves and the hips that give a woman a beautiful stature, it's simply attitude because when you have the right attitude people find you attractive irrespective of your body contours.

When the mother of the young girl who had an unclean spirit came to Jesus she came with hope that her little girl would be healed. Unfortunately she was a Gentile and Jesus told her that he needed to feed the Jews first. If she had had a rotten attitude she would have stormed away and cursed but not this woman. Her attitude was in place. She was not moved by what she initially heard and she knew the one with whom she spoke. So in her defense she pointed out to Jesus that even the crumbs of his grace would be good enough for her. What an attitude. Jesus was so moved he had no choice but give this woman the miracle she wanted.

The power of a good positive attitude can do for you the impossible.

Psalm 54:^{22}-Cast your burden on the Lord and he shall sustain you; He shall never permit the righteous to be moved

Bible Reference:

Matthew 15 verse 21- 28

CHAPTER 7

'The princess within you'

She was just an orphan girl, who was living an ordinary life, even though she was beautiful and was graced with a noted curvy figure. To Mordecai she was already a princess but that is because Mordecai loved her as his own daughter and always saw the best in her.

When Esther was hand-picked to be amongst those women to be chosen to replace Vashti, it was her appointed time and her season to be elevated to another level in life.

What does this Esther have to do with you? Well, you may look like not much to many people at the moment, but your opportune time to be revealed is at hand. You have come this far and have always been in the shadows of others seemingly better than yourself.

Be sure of this, you are of the right colour, of the right nationality and you are exactly in the right place to discover that you are no ordinary woman. You are royalty and very precious in the eyes of God.

Esther had to undergo beauty treatments and be coached on how to conduct herself before the king.

These are essential for every woman. Get rid of the low self-esteem and come to the place where you are confident in your own skin. Walk gracefully with the poise of a woman who knows her true identity. Rid yourself of any air of arrogance which so easily chokes the grace you are meant to exude as a woman of virtue. A queen or princess does not try too hard to be elegant, they are just so. It is natural to them.

Allow yourself to be pampered by the grace of God that has appeared to all men teaching us to say no to ungodliness. You are beautiful and you are a wonder to behold. As you step out into purpose, find pleasure in what you are doing and do it heartily with the sophistication that has been bestowed upon your life.

You are royalty, hand-picked by God for His own good pleasure. Woman, you are precious and you have found favour in the eyes of the King of glory. Irrespective of where you are or have been, you are accepted. Irrespective of the odds that are against you, the way has been prepared for you. Know for certain that no weapon formed against you shall prosper. Weapons may be formed but it's a guarantee they will not destroy you.

This is your season to put on the crown and you need to seize this opportunity and begin to fulfill the destiny for which you have been preparing since the day you entered into this world.

Princess, the royal scepter of God's favour has been pointed in your direction…God is ready and more than willing to give you what you are about to ask Him.

Luke 1:[28]-Rejoice, highly favoured one, the Lord is with you; blessed are you among women

Bible Reference:
Esther 1 verse 19, 2 verse 5 – 8, 5 verses 2 -3
Titus 2 verse 11, Isaiah 54 verse 17

CHAPTER 8

"I need a massage"

When you take the time to refresh others you yourself will be refreshed one day.

Every act of kindness, though it can be hidden from the accolades of men, will one day be rewarded. Usually the rewards of our acts of kindness come when we least expect.

Oftentimes it looks as if you are being taken for granted, never getting the appreciation you deserve. What you need to keep in mind is that there is one who keeps a score of every good deed you do and He vouches that none of it will go unnoticed and unrewarded.

Sometimes you went out of your way to help those who were in need. Other times you sacrificed your time and resources to make sure the one in need could be comforted.

You have always given your best and never asked for anything in return. Yet you wonder …when you need help the most, it seems as if you are all alone. When you need a helping hand, it seems everyone else is too busy to help.

You are a woman with a golden heart and even if you do not get the river of thank-you-s flowing towards you, continue to do good and to be kind.

Today know it in your heart that you are making a difference in individuals and if the individual is responsible enough, you are touching families. Significance starts by small acts of kindness. While many are laboring to be successful you are becoming significant. You are making an impact and your acts of kindness will outlive you and precede the next generation.

You may not become the most prominent among women, but your impact on mankind will forever be ingrained on the hearts of many as you touch families one by one.

Begin where you are, to become significant. Start with a smile, a gentle touch or a kind word. These resources are always at your disposable and the more of it you give the more you'll discover greater wealth within yourself to enrich others.

The day you wish and say, "I need a massage", do not be surprised to find a dozen hands ready to give you that good longed for massage.

Proverbs 21:21- Whoever pursues righteousness and love finds life, prosperity and honour

CHAPTER 9

"It can't be another bad hair day!"

The battle was never meant to be yours but you made it your own.

You are highly commended for what you have been through and have come out strong. For every tear you have shed and every heart-ache you have suffered and endured, other women will salute you because you never gave up.

Life threw in your face all kinds of situations and dilemmas and in all these, though at times you were in tears, you never gave up, you stood your ground. You were even prepared to die for love, because you thought it was a cause that was worth every ounce of effort in you.

Many times you stood alone and pressed on alone, but listen, the battle was never meant to be yours. God never meant for your hair to be ruffled that's why He promised to never leave you nor forsake you.

Your place is and has always been to fight the good fight of faith, to hold on to the promises of God irrespective of the raging war.

From today going forward, meet whatever comes your way with calm and tranquility within. Let that peace come from knowing that you are not alone.

In the book of Daniel, it is declared that the people who know their God will be strong and do mighty exploits. You are that people and your very inner fortitude comes through knowing that the Lord Almighty God is on your side through eternity.

The three Hebrew boys faced the fiery furnace with resolute conviction that their God was in control – and they declared – that even if their God was not going to save them from the burning flames – they were not going to bow down to the statue and the penalty for such a stance against the king was carried out.

God will never put you to shame. King Nebuchadnezzar leaped to his feet in amazement and asked if they had not just thrown three men in the blazing furnace. Almighty God was on the scene, in the fire with his beloved and the flames could not dare touch them. What victory!

When the battle rages on, keep that hair- do, no need to fret and squirm, keep the faith and declare your victory, because the battle belongs to God.

Proverbs 3:[5] -Trust in the Lord with all your heart and lean not on your own understanding; [6]in all your ways acknowledge him and he will make your paths straight

Bible Reference:

Hebrews 13 verse 5
1 Timothy 6 verse 12
Daniel 11 verse 32
Daniel 3 verse 10 – 18, 2

CHAPTER 10

'Dub some blush on those cheeks'

SOmetimes, as a woman, the day takes a toll on you but guess what, it was never meant to be that way.

Yes as a woman you can have a thousand things glaring in your face all wanting a bit, if not all, of your attention. When you find yourself in this predicament, prioritize and do what you need to do from position of rest. Simply put;

- Have a schedule
- Prioritize
- Delegate
- Give total attention to the task at hand
- Manage time well and
- Don't let others waste your time

Be wise enough to acknowledge everything that you have to do but in the process of acknowledging it, don't let it overwhelm you. The idea is to plan by prioritizing and that way you get on top on your game.

Never allow your duties and responsibilities to dictate to you how your day should unfold, learn the art of doing what you have to do, and all you have to do, the smart way.

Blush helps to make your face glow and look alive and that is just what you need in your daily tasks. Apply some blush of enthusiasm and it will make you alive as you do the hundreds of things, one at a time.

Application is fairly straightforward - simply put a smile on your face and see each task as a joy and that will boost your enthusiasm level.

Don't complicate things. Just as make-up blush should match your natural skin color, make enthusiasm come from inside you. Let it blend in with your attitude.

Ecclesiastes 9:10 beautifully puts it across when it says, 'whatever your hand finds to do, do it with all your might.'

So really whatever you have to do, no matter how small or big, significant or trivial, just do it with a touch of enthusiasm.

Dorcas had so much enthusiasm that she spent all her time doing good and helping the poor. Her life was like a magnet of love that when she died the people could not bury her. Instead they called the apostle to come and give this woman another chance to live. There was evidence of her love and that love came from the spring of enthusiasm flowing in her veins. Her passion worked out her miracle because Dorcas was raised from the dead and one can only imagine the joy that filled her heart as she continued living doing good from a bubbly spirit.

Remember real beauty comes from the heart and you will always be beautiful inside and out. Should you not get a thank-you for all you do, keep the smile, it's okay because God promises that your labours of love are not in vain.

Colossians 3:23 – and whatever you do, do it heartily, as to the Lord…

Bible Reference:

Acts 9 verse 36 – 41
1 Corinthians 15 verse 58

CHAPTER 11

'Remove the frown from your brow'

It is said that the number one cause of having a wrinkled face in your prime years is frowning too much. How true that is may be questionable, but a frown on a face of a beautiful woman like you, is definitely unbecoming.

When you consider that you were made in God's very image, the thought of this miracle itself should be powerful enough to erase any frown from your brow. You might not hear it often but God engaged His creativity to make a woman. Why then should you frown when you were so carefully knit together while you were in your mother's womb?

Mary was just a woman like any one of us. Yes, undeniably, she was privileged to be the mother of the Lord Jesus Christ, but just like most women she had her share of her inner pain. Mary totally surrendered herself to God and found her joy in honouring God with her obedience. When Mary meets with Martha she breaks forth in praise, her heart oozing with gratitude that she could not contain.

Special woman, you don't need to be poetic, for gratitude can be expressed in the most simple of words, "thank you." If you insist on being poetic about gratitude, it still remains fairly simple, "thank you, thank you, very much!"

Many times women all over the world fail to be grateful because their focus is all wrong. They focus on what they don't have or on what they are expecting and trusting God for. Choose to be different and focus on what you already have and what God has already done for you. Count your blessing one by one, irrespective of what your circumstances may be. As you go through each circumstance and situation refuse to focus on the negative but rather determine in your heart to be grateful. Always have this conviction - you are not alone - the Lord will never leave you nor will He forsake you.

Remove that frown from your brow. It's unbecoming for a woman like you. Rather be grateful and put on the garment of praise for that way you are guaranteed to reap even more joy than you can imagine.

Ephesians 5:^{20} - Always giving thanks to God the Father in everything …

Bible Reference:

Luke 1 verse 34 – 35, 38, 46-55

CHAPTER 12

'Is there a ring on your finger?'

Whether it's a wedding band, an engagement ring or a fashion ring, it's important that you have a ring adorning your fingers. A ring is symbolic. It is a circle that has neither a beginning nor an end. It is symbolic of commitment.

Hannah was childless and it ached her heart daily, especially with the taunting remarks she was not spared by Peninnah. One day at the temple Hannah cried her heart out to the point that the priest thought she was drunk. To such an unfair assumption by the priest, Hannah replied, "I am a woman who is deeply troubled… I have been raving here out of my great anguish and grief".

During this agonistic prayer hour Hannah vowed, made a commitment to God, that if the Lord answered her, she would give her son (the one she was praying for) to the Lord for all the days of his life.

In the fullness of time God fulfilled Hannah's prayer and Hannah in turn fulfilled her vow and took her gift, her son, to the house of the Lord.

There are commitments you made in your life as a wife, a mother, a daughter, a sister or just as a child of God. You may not have been as dramatic as Hannah was, but you committed yourself and therefore you must honour your commitment because you are a woman of character.

You need to realize just how important it is for you to honour your commitment. You are a woman of character, despite your lapses here and there. If for some reason or another you had removed your ring from your finger, put it back in its rightful finger.

Commit yourself to being the best you;

Commit yourself to your family;

Commit yourself to your passions and dreams;

Commit yourself to living life like today was your last day on earth;

Commit yourself to God.

Is there a ring on your finger? You are a special woman and the answer to this question should be, "yes there is."

Psalm 37:^{5} – Commit your way to the Lord, trust in Him and He will do this.

Bible Reference:

1 Samuel 1verse 8 – 28

CHAPTER 13

"Mirror, mirror on the wall..."

"Mirror, mirror, on the wall, who's the fairest of them all?" To this question the magic mirror replies that there is another woman out there more beautiful than her.

Unfortunately this magic mirror in the fairytale truthfully replies the woman asking the question and tells her there is another woman out there more beautiful than her. It makes her furious.

So you might not be asking the magic mirror directly but how do you look at the other women in your circle of life.

Is there a woman more beautiful than you, more educated than you, more successful in business than you, more elegant than you or seemingly more blessed than you?

Yes, of course there is! This is because you are comparing yourself to her and yet you are two different women.

You need to see yourself from the lenses of God's eyes. You can never compare yourself to another woman because you are unique, and, believe it or not, you have no idea what the other woman may be wishing she had in her life.

The apostle Paul, in his letter to the church in Philippi, wrote: I have learned in whatever state I am to be content.

You can learn to be content if you are not already content.

Look in the mirror and see yourself. Contentment is simply being quietly satisfied with who you are and what you have. It is accepting God's care and provision. Contentment is great gain because it stops you from comparing yourself to others, stops you from being envious and from being judgmental.

The next time you stand in front of your mirror and decide to chant – your chant should sound more like – "mirror, mirror on the wall who's the fairest of them all?" to which the mirror of your heart will reply: "you are, because you are content and you are in a league of your own."

Hebrews 13:[5] - be content with such things as you have. For He Himself has said, I will never leave you nor forsake you.

Bible Reference:

Philippians 4 verse 11

CHAPTER 14

"Make sure everything is perfect"

As a woman never throw clothes on yourself just to cover up your body...wear your clothes!

It really does not matter how big and wide your walk-in closet is, or whether your clothes are kept in a suitcase; the moment you decide to put some clothes on your body make sure you wear the clothes and not just throw them on.

Take pride in how you dress. If it is just the one blouse, make sure it's clean and not creased unless the crease is the design of the fabric. If it's the one suit for work, make sure it looks perfect as if it's from the dry-cleaners.

Allow your body the pleasure and luxury of clean clothes daily, irrespective of where you are going or what you are doing. Even if your task for the day is a bit messy, don't have a care- less attitude. How you wear your clothes reflects who you are and your clothes should always compliment your body.

When it was Esther's turn to appear before the king, Esther requested nothing but what Hegai, the king's eunuch, the custodian of the women, advised. Hegai understood what appealed to the king and he proudly dressed and adorned Esther to the king's liking, which made Esther walk on the red carpet of royalty as the new queen.

Your attention to your clothes will open doors for you which otherwise would remain closed.

Why is this so important? As earlier mentioned it's simply because your dressing reflects how you feel about yourself inside. Remember it's not about quantity. Aim for perfection.

Perfection is parallel to being complete in Christ Jesus.

Let it be true for you that your life is hidden with Christ in God. If it be so, then perfection is your lifestyle. You don't do things in half measures. You go all out for perfection. Christ has already perfected you so take your rightful place.

Wear your clothes with the exuding confidence of a woman who knows her true identity. If you need royal advise, from one who understands what appeals to the king, Hegai is always there with you and your Hegai is no other than the Holy Spirit Himself. He will adorn you as you wear your clothes. As you become more mature, being fully developed and complete, perfection will be your second-nature. You will be a symbol of perfection just as God meant it to be for you.

Hold your head high and walk with confidence knowing that you do not walk alone.

Hebrews 6:[1] - "…therefore leaving the discussion of the elementary principles of Christ, let us go on to perfection…"

Bible Reference:
Esther 2 verse 15, Colossians 3 verse 3

CHAPTER 15

'Rest will rejuvenate you!'

It's easy to neglect yourself over and over again as you keep procrastinating everything you have to do to take care of yourself. You make the sacrifices to do what you need to do for everybody else and before you know it the day is finished and you have not paid attention to your needs.

It may take days, or weeks or even months until you come to realize that you have actually been neglecting the most important person in the world – you!

One of the symptoms of self-neglect is fatigue. In extreme cases bags form under your eyes. Put lightly, but frankly, your face begins to show signs of ageing. Irrespective of how old you are, it seems, age wrinkles you overnight.

Two sisters, Mary and Martha, loved Jesus but they sure had different ways of showing it.

Mary, easy-going, sat at the feet of Jesus and heard his words while, busy-body, Martha, on the other hand could not be still but was distracted with much serving.

Unfortunately and sadly, Martha was not at rest while she served. She actually had a problem with Mary not helping her to the extent she blurted it out, in accusatory tones, to Jesus. Jesus sensed the turmoil in Martha and calmly spoke to her, "Martha, Martha" (how refreshing), "you are worried and troubled about many things, but one thing is needed…"

It's not the serving, making sure everyone is comfortable, that the children are well-fed, that the house is tidy, that the clothes are washed and ironed, that the dog has been fed and that the cat has a rat to chase…

One thing is needed…and that is you find a time and place to rest. All you need is to just sit down and be still in the presence of your Lord and saviour. You can be assured of one thing…the world will not crush over your head because you stopped serving. Actually if you don't stop and rest, you are the one who will crush under the unmerciful burden of fatigue.

Pamper yourself with rest. Rest within your spirit and in your mind. Surrender every concern and worry to the one who is able to do something about it. Cast all your care on Jesus for he cares for you.

Let go of every care and rest in his presence. His words will rejuvenate you and by the time you get up, you will not need to chase your tail again. You will do what you need to do, not with a sigh, but with a smile on your face.

One thing is needed…rest…because you need it.

Matthew 11:[28] – Jesus said, 'Come to me all you who labour and are heavy laden and I will give you rest.'

Bible Reference:

Luke 10 verse 38 - 42
1 Peter 5 verse 7

CHAPTER 16

'From a nobody to somebody'

In 1Peter 2:10 the bible says that "once you were not a people but now you are people belonging to God…" It's among God's specialty to transform nobodies into prominent people.

So it may be true that right now your life is stagnant and barren so to speak. There is really nothing happening that you can talk loud about, let alone boast about. Maybe you are in a good place because if there was something you could boast about who knows how pompous and caught up in the air you would be.

The beauty of allowing God to make you someone is that the platform of your success will be nothing other than the grace of God in your life. When He makes you, on the basis of His unmerited favour, then you are positioned to re-direct all glory back to Him.

Just because you have nothing spectacular happening in your life right now does not mean there is nothing spectacular inside you. God did not create you without purpose. The purpose He placed inside you is as glorious as the one who placed it in you. So it's true there is nothing happening but pause for a moment and consider the following:
When a tree is planted do we see its fruit before its maturity?

When a woman is carrying child does the stomach just pop out the day the child is conceived?

You are a wise woman and you definitely answered 'no' to the above questions. So there you are! Just because there is no evident fruit right now, that does not mean there is nothing happening inside you right now. The nothingness you sense is awareness that something magnificent is happening within you and before long, this very woman who thought she was nobody will be something to talk about. You will have a testimony alright, and keep in mind that, God is working it all out for you so that His name may be glorified in and through your life.

Consider the widow Elisha helped out of a predicament. This widow comes to Elisha in tears and tells him that the creditor is coming to take her two sons away from her. Elisha is sympathetic and asks, "What do you have in the house?" Just pause for a moment: there is always something in your house or in your life that is a seed to your breakthrough, but if you allow the tears of self-pity to blur your vision, you will miss it completely. In response the widow said, "-nothing…" Really! No! "Nothing but a jar of oil"

Woman, you have something. That jar of oil is all you need for your breakthrough. That little something which you are looking at as insignificant, is all you need to become everything God wants you to become. Your key to success and victory is in your house. Your house figuratively speaking, is yourself.

'Nothing but this'. It is 'this' the 'something', that will take you as far as you want to go in life.

Psalm 84:^{11} For the Lord God is a sun and shield; the Lord will give grace and glory; no good thing will He withhold from those who walk uprightly

Bible reference

2 kings 4:1-7

CHAPTER 17

'Express the real you'

It is sad how adults can lose the innocence of their childhood years when everything and anything was possible. When everything was pure and lots of fun. When the only limits they knew, but rebelled against, were those set by their parents.

As a little girl you were like a canvas on which every day you painted an abstract picture with passion and enthusiasm. You instinctively had the vibe to dance when the music played and the joy to giggle at everything or nothing. As a little girl you were a bundle of joy and always on the move…and then…

Then you became a woman and everything seemed to change. You no longer saw yourself from the lenses of your own eyes but began to see yourself from the lenses of the world. You wanted the world to accept you and you wanted to fit in but you never really did. To avoid hurting yourself you stopped dancing to the music in your life and stopped painting the abstract paintings everyday…you conformed and eventually lost yourself.

The reason why you are not really happy is because you are not being true to yourself. There is the person, inside you, who is longing to come out and be all that she can be. You do not need to deny yourself the opportunity to live life….really live life. Right now is the moment of reality. Right now you can laugh and hear your own voice. Right now you can get up and start dancing to that music that always plays deep inside you. Right now you have the chance of a lifetime to become truly the woman God created you to be. The woman who believes that all things are possible and there are no limits except the ones you put for yourself.

One day the Syrians went out and brought back a captive young woman from the land of Israel and she served Naaman's wife. Despite being in captivity upon seeing Naaman, she found her voice and spoke up that in Samaria there was a prophet who could cure Naaman of his leprosy. She could have kept quiet and denied herself the chance to express who she really was and Naaman would have remained a leper. Not this young lady. She spoke and in so doing brought salvation to a man of national influence.

When you express the real you, you not only bring salvation to the people around you, but you find greater fulfillment in life. Your circumstances are not the limiting factor. The limiting factor right now is your unwillingness and your refusal to express the person God made you to be.

Rise up and find your voice. The world is waiting for a vivacious woman like you to bring some zest into life.

Matthew 5:[14] –You are the light of the world.

Bible Reference:

2 Kings 5 verses 2 -3

CHAPTER 18

"Water is good for your health"

A dehydrated body is no good for a woman who wants to be forever beautiful. Maybe your beauty is fading away because you are dehydrated emotionally as a result of rejection.

Rejection comes in all forms from any direction. It may be that your husband left you for another woman and now you stare in the mirror and see all your flaws. You blame yourself over and over again only to wrench your heart with pain.

Maybe your boyfriend left you when you had plans for a future with him. Maybe he cheated on you but you did not handle it okay. Maybe it's not even about men, but it's one of your sisters – who shut you out.

Rejection is never easy, whether it's being divorced, being cheated on, being dumped or simply being ignored by someone. Rejection makes a woman feel as if she is not good enough and she does not measure up.

The Samaritan woman by the well seemed to have had some experience with rejection but somehow in her own way she managed to pick herself up and give herself chance after chance. This woman seemed to never give up on herself and refused to be battered by rejection. When Jesus in time meets with her by the well, she is now on her sixth man. Jesus could have condemned this woman, but it is not like Jesus to do so. Instead he reaches out to her and offers her the living water.

Take notice that this woman was not beat up with a low self-esteem or self-pity. She could have been conscious of how people around her looked at her but she went about her daily tasks. She had a care-free attitude towards rejection.

During her conversation with Jesus at one point she says, "Sir, I perceive that you are a prophet." Later on she acknowledges that indeed Jesus was the true Messiah.

You need to stop where you are and become aware that you are a special woman and that Jesus, loves you very much. Don't beat yourself up because someone walked out of your life, shut the door in your face or sneaked behind your back. No. Take your jar and go to the well and drink of the living water. In fact the Lord promised that he will give you living water and you will never thirst again.

God is not limited at all. His love is more than enough to restore all you lost and fill the emptiness inside you. As you hide yourself in the bosom of the Almighty God, he will surely cause you to find real love that you will never thirst again.
Drink your water, it will guarantee you eternal beauty!

John 7:[37 -38] Jesus said: if anyone thirsts, let him come to me and drink. He who believes in me...out of his heart will flow rivers of living water

Bible Reference:

John 4 verses 7 – 26

CHAPTER 19

'A lady's handbag is very personal'

The contents of a woman's handbag are as essential and as personal to her as it can get. It has been alleged by some that you can define a woman by what you find in her handbag.

A plain woman will not carry a lipstick, eyebrow pencil or mascara in her handbag, whereas another woman will not leave the house without her make-up bag in her handbag.

Make-up or no make-up, every woman should have a handbag and there are essentials that are a must in that handbag.

As a woman, among your essentials, you need your love, joy, peace, patience, kindness, goodness and your self-control.

The first time Elisha went to Shunem, he met a woman who persuaded him to stay for a meal. It became a habit, thereafter, that each time Elisha went to Shunem, he ate at the woman's house. After a while the woman spoke to her husband that they should build a room and furnish it comfortably so that the man of God could stay there whenever he visited Shunem.

These acts of kindness and expression of love made Elisha enquire about this woman's desires. He was told she was a blessed woman, except that she did not have any children. On hearing this, Elisha, the man of God, made a promise to the woman that she would be blessed with a son and as per his word, a year later this virtuous woman became a mother.

As you carry your handbag everywhere you go, in the same way, let love and faithfulness never leave you. Bind them around your heart, write them on the tablet of your heart. Love is an essential for every woman. No matter who you are, where you are and what you have, without love life is meaningless.

You do not love so that you get something in return. You love because love is the glue that glues every piece of the puzzle of life together. You love because love is of God and you know God and are born of God and God first loved you.

Carry some love around for the world is in desperate need of sincere godly love that only a woman like you can give freely and unconditionally.

Numbers 6: 24-25 – The Lord bless you and keep you; the Lord make his face shine upon you

Bible References:

Galatians 5 verse 22
2 Kings 4 verse 8 – 17
Proverbs 3 verse 3
1 John 4 verse 7 – 8

CHAPTER 20

"Take care of your man!"

If you are married, engaged or dating then this is for you. Your man's joy and satisfaction is your responsibility. How far you go is determined by the nature of your relationship, but if you are married, you have to go all out as far as romantic intimacy.

Much as you are a daughter of Sarah, and call your man lord! lord! Have an understanding why your man was attracted to you in the first place. If you have lost your touch of love that made your man madly in love with you on the first day, then, take a deep breath, close your eyes and breathe out. You need to rekindle that love or else Deliah will find her way to your man.

Deliah's love portion is nothing but her understanding of knowing what soothes a man. Samson was lulled to sleep by Deliah's sweet voice and it gave the Philistines the opportunity to cut off his hair. Samson lost his relationship with God, his anointing and his power just because a woman pleased him. You may be the first lady now but if Deliah lulls your man and makes him feel like superman, then you will kiss your first- lady -position good-bye.

Let your man be yours alone and be his completely. Let your eyes shine with love and your cheeks glow with joy of being in his presence. Let the look in your eyes steal his heart and allow your love to delight him.

Your man wants to smell your fragrance on your clothing. He wants to hear you tell him how strong and handsome he is. He wants to know that everything about him enchants you and that you are proud of him.

Quit telling your man that he is a good for nothing. Quit comparing your man with the man next door. Stop reminding him of his weaknesses which, by the way, he is already aware of.

Most beautiful woman, where has your lover gone?

Don't let him go to Deliah.

Follow him to his garden where he is feeding his flocks. Watch him and let your eyes hold him captive by their admiration of him. Make him tremble with desire and eager for love.

You belong to your man and let him know that with him you find contentment and peace.

Be your man's companion, cheerleader and lover even if it means lavishing him with all the sweet words he wants to hear.

Songs of Solomon 2:^{15} -Catch the little foxes before they ruin your vineyard in bloom

Bible Reference:

Judges 16 verse 4, 19 -20
1 Peter 3 verse 6

CHAPTER 21

'Use your words to create your world'

In the very beginning the earth was without form and empty and the Spirit of God was hovering over the waters. He was ready for action but He could not act just yet.

What was the spirit of God waiting for? The Spirit of God was waiting for the spoken word. The plan of creation had already been set in motion but could not be executed without the spoken word.

Immediately as the words were being released from the mouth of God, let there be light...creation took place...and there was light.

The word had to be released for creation to take place.

What plans do you have for your life that you have strategized in your mind? What plans do you have for your family? What do you want to create?

Your plans need a voice. You must begin to say things that you want to create in your life. Death and life are in the power of the tongue. God has given you the power to create whatever you want – but that power can only be released by words. Use your words to create the life you want.

Jabez, although born inferior to his brothers, stumbled upon this truth and used it to create for himself a life of abundance and success. Jabez was one of those guys who you could pity just by hearing his name. His name meant pain because his mother had borne him out of pain. He was a pain in the neck for his mother. When Jabez became aware of the truth that God was willing and prepared to honour his words, he changed his talk and he called out to God and said – 'oh that you would bless me indeed and enlarge my territory, that your hand would be with me and that you would keep me from evil and that I may not cause pain!'

Even though it was a mouthful, God granted him his request. If you speak it, God will create it for you if it's not already there.

God needs us to pray things into existence. He designed us to say things and through saying things to create. We create our life by the words we speak. You channel the destinies of your children by the words you speak in their life. You have authority to create whatever you will by your words. Never underestimate the power of the words that you speak. By the words of your mouth you shall eat of the land.

Proverbs 18[20] - From the fruit of their mouth a person's stomach is filled; with the harvest of their lips they are satisfied.

Bible Reference:

Genesis 1 verse 2
1 Chronicles 4 verses 9 – 10

CHAPTER 22

'Looking back over your shoulder'

This is how far you have come in life and so much has happened and yet here you are still looking forward to tomorrow or are you dreading what tomorrow holds for you.

For you – it may be that when you remember what the Lord has done, there is no way that you can go back anymore.

For another woman it may be – you need to start a new walk with Christ Jesus because the past has offered you nothing but pain.

Wherever you are in life, it takes courage to appreciate that you are where you are, because this small appreciation offers you an opportunity to take the next step forward.

When Anna looked over her shoulder – her past dashed before her eyes in a flash like lighting. She was a virgin when she got married and she sparkled with joy in her home. She was a wife for seven years before death knocked at her door and claimed the life of her husband. Seven years of marriage and it was all over. Unexpectedly she was now a young widow. After mourning her husband, Anna realized that no other man could ever replace the man she had loved so much and lost so early, so she devoted her life to prayer.

At eighty four years old, Anna looks over her shoulder one more time and this time, she is in the temple. A prophetess, who had all these years after the death of her husband, been serving God with prayers and fastings and had never left the temple since then. Now Anna stands and bears witness to the birth of the promised redeemer. Could it be that all these years she was waiting for the fulfillment of the promised Messiah? If so, her years of ministry and waiting were rewarded as she witnessed baby Jesus being dedicated in the temple.

What do you see when you look over your shoulder? Are there memories of pain and tears that you'd rather not talk about? Are there moments of joy that you will cherish for the rest of your life?

Whatever it may be, remember you are who you are today because of what happened in the past. If it's a past you want to forget about, remember there is a redeemer, the Lord Jesus, who is willing and ready to usher you into newness of life. If it's a past you will forever cherish, remember, the Lord in his faithfulness has brought you this far and He will continue with you to the very end.

The idea is not to walk looking over your shoulder. His desire is for you to walk through life with your eyes fixed on Jesus. His desire is for you to skip in the meadows of happy moments, and wade through the path of trial with your head held up, confident that you are not alone.

Psalm 23[4] - Even though I walk through the darkest valley I will fear no evil, for you are with me; your rod and your staff, they comfort me.

Bible Reference:
Luke 2 verse 36 – 38, Hebrews 12 verse 2

CHAPTER 23

"It's not your lot to be bent over"

Remember the days when you used to walk tall and could see the world beyond the horizon. The hue colours of the sunset used to dazzle you with their natural beauty. You did not realize it when you stopped to watch the sunset because you could not stand up tall anymore.

You managed to tolerate the discomfort of walking bend over because initially it was the most comfortable position to walk in, considering the burden you had to bear. You desperately wanted the freedom to walk tall but circumstances prevented you and you accepted it. What you did not realize is that your new position shriveled your spirit and with it came helplessness and bitterness. You allowed yourself to become a victim of pain and discomfort until now!

Now a woman, having a flow of blood for twelve years, who had spent all her livelihood on doctors and could not be healed by any, came from behind and touched Jesus by the hem of his garment. Immediately she was healed.

For twelve years this woman had walked bend over with an ailment that could not be cured, rejection from society, physical uncleanness and the burden of shame. When Jesus was passing through the town, she revolved to go to Jesus, but she was aware that she was so unworthy to be in his presence. Her decision then, was that she would only make contact with his clothes and that would be good enough for her.

Pressing through the crowd she managed to touch the hem of His garment and according to her faith, she was instantly healed but that did not go unnoticed by the healer. Despite the throng around him, Jesus felt his power being pulled by the faith of this woman and to the astonishment of his disciples he asked who had touched him.

Jesus is your burden- bearer and he wants to lift that burden that has made you bent over with shame and discouragement. It does not really matter how heavy the burden is. When you go on your bended knees you are closer to the one who can lift that burden. Jesus wants to heal your spirit and straighten you up. Reach out to Jesus as you bow your knee before him. When his power connects with your faith, your healing will be made manifest immediately.

Ephesians 3^{20} – now to Him who is able to do exceedingly abundantly above all that we ask or think, according to the power that works in us, to Him be glory

Bible Reference:

Mark 5 verse 25 – 34

CHAPTER 24

"Affirm who you are from A to Z"

A

I am **anointed** and therefore whatever I put my hands to do prospers and flourishes like cedars of Lebanon.

I am **able** to accomplish great and mighty things and leave a legacy and an inheritance for my children and my children's children.

I am **abounding** in grace as I draw from the overflow of God's grace that is evident in my life.

I am **abounding** in hope therefore no circumstance and no situation can get the best of me.

I am **accepted** in the beloved. Jesus accepts me the way I am, with or without any make-up.

I have **access** in Christ Jesus, access to victory and strength, access to abundance and every good things that pertains to life and godliness.

I am **adequate**, made whole and lacking nothing. All that I need and will ever need, God has already placed inside me.

I am **adopted** and are now called by a new name – God's beloved.

I am **alive** and in Him I move, live and have my being.

I am an **ambassador** of the good news that Jesus loves and cares. I am His ambassador to proclaim to the nations that He is the Way, the Truth and the Life.

I am **anxious for nothing** because He supplies all my needs according to His riches in Christ Jesus.

I am the **aroma** of Christ. My life is a fragrance that perfumes the atmosphere around me.

I am the **apple of His eye** therefore nobody and nothing can touch my life without drawing the attention of the Lord my God.

I am **appointed** by God and no one has the power to revoke that appointment.

I am **not ashamed** simply because I am clothed with His righteousness and beautified by His grace.

I am **assured of reward** so all my labour of love is never in vain. God is no woman's debtor.

I am **assured of success** in every area of my life. All I need to do, is do the word and leave the results to God.

I have **authority** over satan and no devil has power to terrorize me or linger in my territory.

B

I am **baptized** into Christ, washed by His precious blood and completely cleansed.

I am **beautiful** without comparison, unique and a jewel in the eyes of God.

I am **becoming a mature** person daily as I seek His face and have fellowship with Him.

I am a **believer** who trusts and holds on to God's word without any doubt.

I **belong** to God and nobody and nothing will snatch me out of His hands.

I am **blameless,** with no condemnation and no accusation can be brought towards me. He paid the price for me in full.

I am **blessed** so much that those without what I have wonder how I do it.

I am **blood bought** by the precious blood of Jesus.

I am **bold** like the lion of the tribe of Judah

I am a **bondservant**, pledged to serve no other except Jesus Christ, the One who alone is worthy.

I am **born again** – a new creation – the past has gone and behold all things have become new.

I am **bough**t with a price unmatched by any man

I am a **branch** abiding in the vine.

I am his **bride** being perfected every day for His glory and pleasure.

I am **brought near** so that I daily live under His divine protection where the devil can do me no harm.

I am **built up** in Christ Jesus to the full measure of my potential in order that I might do the great works He prepared for me beforehand.

I am **buried** with Christ therefore it is no longer I who lives but Christ lives in me .

C

I am **called** by name. He knows all my going out and coming in.

I am **cared for** with an unconditional love, unlimited favour and tremendous grace upon grace.

I am **carried** on His wings allowing me to soar like an eagle above all the calamities and storms of life.

I am **changed** every moment to conform to His perfect image by having my mind renewed by His word.

I am a **child of God**, born not of the corruptible seed but of the incorruptible seed.

I am **cherished** by the Father and He loves me dearly with an everlasting love.

I am **chosen**, handpicked by the God Almighty not because I am wise or I am good in myself but simply because He chose me to be His.

I am **circumcised** spiritually not with the circumcision of man. It's my heart that has been circumcised as a symbol of my sanctification.

I am a **citizen of heaven**, guaranteed to walk on the streets of gold one day and bask in His glorious presence.

I am **clay** in God's hands and He is moulding me as a vessel of honour.

I am **clean**, washed whiter than snow and having no blemish at all as far as He sees me.

I am **clothed** with the robe of righteousness, uniquely tailored to fit me as an individual.

I am **co-heir** with Christ Jesus, therefore what belongs to Christ Jesus is mine to enjoy as well.

I am **comforted**

I am complete in Christ, nothing to be added and nothing to be subtracted.

I am **confident** to lift my head high and walk tall

I am **conformed to Christ** and not to this world because though I am in this world I am really not of this world

I am a **conqueror**, no, that is an understatement. I am more than a conqueror.

I am **content** with who I am and what I have.

I am **continually with** God who has pledged to never leave me nor forsake me.

I am **controlled by** God's love which is a far better way to live my life.

I am **courageous** to live my life to the full and meet every challenge head on. What I cannot push, I go over, what I can't go over I go through!

I am **created for good works** which God prepared for me beforehand so that His manifest power is demonstrated through my life.

I am **created** in His image which makes me one with God.

I am **crucified** with Christ; dead to this world therefore sin has no power over me.

I am **confident of answers** to prayer. His ears are attentive to me and He answers me so that my joy is full.

I am **confident** He will never leave me because He said so and that settles it.

D

I am **dead to sin** for I know Him in whom there is no variation or shadow of turning.

I am a **delight** and that's why God enjoys my fellowship and longs to have communion with me every day.

I am **delighted in** by the Lord God and also by those who know me .

I am **delivered** from the kingdom of darkness into His marvelous light.

I am **desired** not only as a companion and a friend but as a mother, a sister and a daughter.

I am **determined** to remain focused on what is important and what really matters. Nothing will deter me from reaching my goals.

I am a **disciple** who is devoted to the Lord Jesus Christ.

I am **disciplined** to hold on to the principles set out in the word of God and holding on to the values of a godly woman.

I **draw near** to God in confidence because I understand and appreciate that Jesus gave me access to the throne room of God Almighty.

E

I am **empowered** to obey His word and walk worthy of His calling.

I am **encouraged** not only so that I am happy on my own but so that I am an oasis at which many who are discouraged are refreshed.

I am **enlightened**, having the eyes of my spirit opened and my ears open to hear the voice of the Shepherd.

I am **enriched** in everything to be a blessing and continue to flourish as an example of what it is to be truly blessed.

I am **equipped** with everything I need to fulfill my calling, live a successful life and achieve all my dreams. The only limitation I have is the one I place on myself.

I am **established**, unmovable, steadfast and holding on to Jesus because I live life from a standpoint of guaranteed victory.

I have **eternal life** so for me to die is gain.

I have **every good thing** happening in my life and coming my way. Goodness follows me all the days of my life.

I am **exalted** at his right hand, sealed with the Holy Spirit who is the guarantee of my position.

F

I am **faithful,** which is a reciprocal response to God's faithfulness in my life.

I am **family** – once I were not a people but now I am God's and have the right to call Him, Abba Father, Daddy.

I am **far from** oppression for all authority has been given to me to trample over snakes and scorpions.

I am **favoured**

I am **filled with joy** which bubbles from within my heart and is highly contagious. Anyone in my presence has no choice but to be joyful.

I am a **first-fruit** of his grace, his mercy and his love.

I am **forgiven** for past, present and future sins.

I am **formed** by God who created my inmost being and delicately knitted me together in my mother's womb.

I was lost but now am **found** and will never leave His presence again.

I am his **fragrance** as I offer my worship and am found in His presence.

I am **free to** dance anywhere and anytime.

I am **freely given** all things to enjoy.

I am a **fellow worker** and it is God who makes everything grow and flourish.

I am **filled with the fruit** of the spirit, love, joy, peace, patience, goodness, faithfulness, kindness, gentleness, and self-control and against such there is no law.

I am **filled with the knowledge** of His will through the wisdom and understanding that the Holy Spirit gives.

G

I am **gifted** and it is through my gifts that I am going to find fulfillment in life.

I am **guiltless** for as far as God is concerned there is no record of wrong against me .

I am **given** His Holy Spirit to be my teacher and the One who guides me into all truth.

I am **guaranteed** an abundant life in Christ Jesus.

I am **glorified** with him and in and through my life He is glorified.

I am **God's child** precious in his sight.

I am **God's gift** to the nations.

I know **God is for me** therefore whosoever messes with me is actually picking a fight with God.

I am **gracious** in my speech, attitude and the way I carry myself.

I am **guarded** by God so He gives angels charge over me so I do not dash my foot against any stone.

I am **guided**, hedged in on the right and on the left. All I need to do is listen to that voice that says, 'here is the way, walk in it'.

I am **given his magnificent** promises and no matter how many they are, they are 'Yes' in Christ to my resounding 'Amen' as they are fulfilled.

H

I am the **head** and not the tail; always above and never under.

I am walking in **health** for no sickness has the power and right to dwell in my body which is God's temple.

I am an **heir** of God and my inheritance is guaranteed.

I am **held by** God and no one will snatch me out of His hand.

I am **hidden** in Christ therefore no danger will befall me. Only from a distance will I see my enemies scattered in defeat.

I am **His** and His alone.

I am his **handiwork** created in Christ Jesus to do good works, which God prepared in advance for me to do

I am **holy** therefore I pursue holiness in word and in deeds

I am **honoured** not only in the sight of God but in the sight of man.

I am **humble** but I know that it does not mean I allow people to walk all over me .

I

I am the **image** of God so I carry myself as one who knows her identity.

I am an **imitator** of Christ, as He is so am I in this world.

I am **in** Christ Jesus

I am **included** in the commonwealth of Israel.

I am **indestructible**. Though this body is daily fading away, my inner man is being renewed daily.

I am **inscribed** on the palm of his hand.

I am **indwelled** by the Holy Spirit; my body is His temple.

J

I am **joyful** always because the joy of the Lord is a never drying fountain within me .

I am **justified** just as if I never sinned.

K

I am **kept** in the loving arms of the LORD my God.

I am **kingdom-minded** for to be carnally minded is death but to be spiritually minded is life in Christ Jesus.

I am **known** by God; He knows all my going out and coming in.

I **know in whom** I have believed and are assured that He will never fail me.

I **know all things** work together for my good, for I love God and have been called according to His purpose.

L

I have **life abundant** which the thief cannot steal, kill or destroy

I have **life** and peace as my mind remains steadfast on Christ.

I am the **light** of the world which cannot be hidden.

I am the **light** in a dark place for I resemble the true light.

I have **life flowing** through me from within my belly.

I **lack no good thing** for I am a woman who seeks the Lord and finds Him.

I am **loved** unconditionally from everlasting to everlasting.

I am **loyal** to the lifter of my head

I am **lavished** with the riches of his grace

M

I am a **magnifier** of God and continually exalt His name.

I am **marked** in him with a seal, the promised Holy Spirit.

I am a **member** of his body functioning according to his purpose in unison with the rest of the body.

I have the **mind** of Christ that understands and accepts divine instruction.

I am a **minister** of the gospel and the message of reconciliation.

I am a **mountain mover** therefore nothing can stand in my way

N

I am **named** by Him and my name is better than precious ointment.

I am **near** to God with a sincere and contrite heart.

I am **never forsaken**, God will not abandon me .

I am **new born,** born to a living hope.

I am a **new creation**, behold all things have become new.

I have **new life** since I have been raised with Christ.

I am **no longer a slave** to sin but a slave to righteousness.

O

I am **obedient** to His teaching.

I have **obtained an inheritance** having been predestined

I am **one** with God being joined with him in spirit.

I am an **over-comer**, overcoming obstacles, fear and trial.

P

I am **pardoned** for the Lord is compassionate towards me .

I am a **partaker of grace** hence no evil can be spoken against me and prevail.

I am a **partaker of his promises,** all his promises which are magnificent and have been fulfilled in Christ

I have **passed from** death to life for I heard and received His word

I am **patient,** unperturbed by circumstances.

I have **peace**, peace that surpasses all understanding; the kind of peace that causes me to have a smile in the midst of storms.

I am being **perfected** in my weaknesses by his grace.

I am **pleasing to** God in all the good I do for others.

I am God's own **possession,** holy and set apart.

I am a **possessor** of all things according to the Abrahamic blessing which is mine in Christ Jesus.

I am **predestined** to conform to the image of Jesus.

I am **prosperous** as blessings are commanded over me and all I put my hands to do prospers.

I have **power over** the devil.

I am **protected** and established in the Lord.

I am **provided for** according to His riches in glory.

I am **purchased,** I am not my own.

I am **purposeful** in all I do according to His plan for me .

Q

I am **qualified** by God and enabled by Him.

R

I am **raised** with Christ having been buried with him.

I have **received mercy** to draw near to the throne of grace with confidence.

I am **redeemed** according to the riches of his grace.

I am always **rejoicing**.

I am **renewed** not only spiritually but physically.

I have **rest** in him to ease from my labours and rejuvenate my soul.

I am **rewarded** according to all I have done.

I am **rooted** and built up in him.

I am **royalty**, crowned with favour and grace.

I am a **royal priesthood,** a holy nation, chosen by God.

S

I am **safe**; the Lord is my refuge, my hiding place.

I am the **salt of the earth** seasoning all with love.

I am **saved** by grace.

I am **sealed** by the Holy Spirit.

I am **seated** with him in heavenly places.

I am **secure** in the land, respected by all men.

I am **set free** from every bondage and addiction.

I am **sharing Christ's inheritance.**

I am his **sheep**; he leads me in green pastures.

I am **sheltered** under his wings.

I am **shielded** by His favour, which ushers me everywhere I go.

I am his **soldier** who does not get caught up in civilian affairs of this world but remains focused on the ultimate goal.

I am **stable** in all my ways.

I am **standing firm** in Christ

I am **strengthened** in him with might.

I am **strong** in the Lord.

I am amply **supplied** in season and out of season.

T

I am the **temple** of the Holy Spirit.

I am **thought about** for God is always mindful of me .

I am **transformed** by the renewing of my mind.

I am **treasured** more than gold, silver and precious stone.

I am **triumphant**, excelling incredibly in all things.

U

I am **unafraid**, courageous to face the present and the future.

I am **understood** by the Lord despite what man may say.

I am **upheld** by his victorious right hand.

I am **upright** walking in the soundness of wisdom.

I am **unblemished** having been cleansed from all impurity.

I have **understanding** which surpasses all my years.

V

I am **valuable** to the extent that He numbers the hair on my head

I live in **victory** and I know no defeat.

W

I am **walking** in the light and enjoying fellowship with others.

I am **washed** having my heart cleaned from an evil conscience.

I am **waiting** for His return, yes I patiently wait.

I am in a **wealthy** place of untold great abundance.

I am a **watered garden** like a spring whose waters never fail.

I am his **witness,** testifying of his goodness and mercy.

I am a **worshipper**, worshipping him in truth and spirit.

X

I am -**Xtra special** – that he declares to all – touch not my anointed.

I am - e**Xtra-ordinary** – I move from glory to glory.

Y

I am **yielded** to God wholly and willingly.

I am **yoked** with Jesus unto righteousness.

Z

I am **zealous**, fervent in spirit, serving the Lord.

I am full of **zest,** life and jubilation, it is simply contagious.

I KNOW WHO I AM

Hallelujah

L et me end by saying,

"*You are beautiful;*

You awe the hearts of many.

You are delightful;

Your life is a fragrance to many.

Yes, charm is deceptive and beauty is fleeting but a woman who fears the Lord is to be praised.

You are that Special Woman.

ABOUT THE AUTHOR

Debbie is the first oldest daughter of Cyril and the late Felistas Gano and she has five young sisters who are on the cover page from youngest to eldest.

She is married to Thobile and has two beautiful daughters, Princess Tsephagalo and Angel Sibongile.

Debbie is a minister of the gospel of Jesus Christ and is founder of IKWIA Ministry. She is currently pastoring at a local children's centre at which she devotes most of her time and resources. Her passion for the Lord Jesus Christ and genuine love for people is what fuels her to do what she does daily to make a difference in the world.

Debbie can be contacted via email – debbiegumede9@gmail.com or +27784776393

Debbie Gumede

www.ingramcontent.com/pod-product-compliance
Lightning Source LLC
Chambersburg PA
CBHW031331040426
42443CB00005B/293